LIFEWATCH

The Mystery of Nature

Caterpillar to Butterfly

Oliver S. Owen

Published by Abdo & Daughters, 4940 Viking Drive, Suite 622, Edina, Minnesota 55435.

Library bound edition distributed by Rockbottom Books, Pentagon Tower, P.O. Box 36036, Minneapolis, Minnesota 55435.

Printed in the United States.

Cover Photo credit: Natural Selection
Interior Photo credits: Natural Selection

Edited By: Bob Italia

LIBRARY OF CONGRESS CATALOGING-IN-PUBLICATION DATA

Owen, Oliver S., 1920-
        Caterpillar to Butterfly / Oliver S. Owen.
                p.   cm. -- (Lifewatch)
        Includes bibliography references (p. 29) and index.
        ISBN 1-56239-290-5
        1. Butterflies--Juvenile literature.   2. Butterflies--Metamorphosis--
        Juvenile literature. [1. Butterflies--Metamorphosis. 2. Metamorphosis.]
        I. Title.   II. Series: Owen, Oliver S., 1920-   Lifewatch.
        QL544.2.095 1994
        595.78'9--dc20   94-14306
                                                                              CIP
                                                                              AC

Contents

The Butterfly 4

The Adult Butterfly 8

Migratory Behavior 14

Mating and Egg Laying 16

The Caterpillar 18

The Pupa 23

Glossary 28

Bibliography 29

Index... 30

The Butterfly

Have you ever watched a butterfly fly from flower to flower? They are the most graceful and beautiful insects on Earth. How did they ever get the name "butterfly"? No one seems to know. There are many thousands of kinds of butterflies in the world. They come in all colors—red, orange, yellow, green, blue, indigo, and violet. The largest butterfly in the world is the *birdwing* butterfly of New Guinea. It has a wingspread of 11 inches! The largest butterfly in the United States is the *tiger swallowtail*.

The tiger swallowtail is the largest butterfly in the United States.

This lovely black and yellow butterfly has a wingtip to wingtip measurement of five inches. Have you seen it fluttering through your flower garden? The smallest butterfly in our country and maybe in the world is the *pygmy blue*. Its wide spread wings would barely cover your fingernail! You perhaps know that birds make long migrations. But so do butterflies! The *monarch* or milkweed butterfly migrates from the northern states all the way south to Texas. That's a flight of about 1,000 miles. But the *painted lady* butterfly does even better. Some of them make the 2,400 mile flight from California to Hawaii!

The smallest butterfly in the United States is the pygmy blue.

How long do butterflies live? Not very long. Some kinds live only a few weeks or months. But a few live to the "ripe old age" of one year. All butterflies pass through several stages of development during their lifetime. This is called metamorphosis—a word which means "change of form." These stages are known as egg, caterpillar, pupa and adult.

Most butterflies fly rather slowly. But some are very fast. The *American copper* is so speedy it can keep up with some birds for a short distance.

Several kinds of butterflies make a sweet juice called honeydew. Some ants love honeydew. So they take care of the honeydew butterflies much like a farmer takes care of his cows. Some caterpillars feed on the leaves of crop plants. They cause millions of dollars of damage every year. However, the adult butterflies are very beneficial. They carry pollen from one flower to another. This makes it possible for the plant to make fruit and seeds. The harm caused by the caterpillars is balanced by the good done by the adult.

Butterflies help plants make fruit and seeds by carrying pollen from one plant to another.

The Adult Butterfly

The butterfly body is divided into three parts—the head, a middle part called the thorax, and a rear part called the abdomen. The butterfly has a pair of two large eyes. However, they are very different from your eyes. If we looked at a butterfly eye with a microscope, we would find that it is made up of up to 20,000 smaller eyes! Such an eye is called a compound eye. Most male butterflies have larger eyes than the female. Therefore, they can see better. This is important because the male has to find a mate. The eyes of the butterflies help them find plants. Their eyes also help them escape from enemies, like flying birds that would like to eat them. Butterflies can see many kinds of colors that you and I cannot! Between the butterfly's eyes are two long, slender antennae. Each antenna has a little knob at the end. (The antennae of moths are feathery and do not have the knobs.)

The butterfly's body has three parts—the head, the thorax, and the abdomen.

This a close-up of a butterfly. Notice the eyes, the antenna, and the furry body.

The antennae serve as the "ears" and "nose" of the butterfly. It uses the antennae to hear and to smell. The antennae help the male and female find each other during courtship. They do this by picking up scents which are given off by the two sexes. The antennae of some butterflies are covered with up to 400 long hairs. They give the butterfly a sense of touch. A slender tube extends down from the face. It is called the proboscis (pro-BOS-is). The

This butterfly is feeding on a plant using its proboscis.

sugary fluid made by flowers, called nectar, is sucked up through the proboscis. (You could watch this action easily by putting a butterfly on a wet cloth smeared with honey.) Some kinds of butterflies do not feed on nectar. Instead, they may feed on rotting fruit and vegetables, tree sap, flower pollen, decaying bodies of mice, urine, solid animal wastes and even human sweat! The most heavily visited butterfly flowers are daisies, mints, mustards, milkweeds and peas. A butterfly spends up to one minute at each flower. When not feeding, the butterfly coils the proboscis under its head like a watchspring.

The butterfly has three pairs of legs. The legs are long, slender and rather weak. The butterfly walks just a few inches with its legs. The legs have many short hairs. Some of these hairs help the female find the right food plant on which to lay her eggs. The legs and feet serve as "tasting" organs. If a flower does not taste right the butterfly will leave. If it tastes good the butterfly will uncoil its proboscis and start feeding.

The two pair of wings are the "crowning glory" of the butterfly. Like the legs, they are also found on the thorax. The wing shape varies greatly among the butterflies. The wings of the *zebra* butterfly are very long and thin. This enables them to be real acrobats. They can fly sideways, backwards and even upside-down! Some butter-flies have triangular wings. In some cases the male has a different wing shape than the female. This makes it easier to find the female.

Notice the way this butterfly coils its proboscis when not feeding.

The nymph butterfly

Notice the differences in the wing pattern of these butterflies.

Indian leafwing butterfly

The gulf fritillary butterfly

The delicate wing is supported by a number of branding "veins." (They do not carry blood as do human veins.) The wings are powered by muscles in the thorax. Most butterflies do not fly over 20 miles per hour. Some butterflies, like monarchs, will glide for several minutes in wind currents. Some can guide themselves during flight with great skill. The zebra butterfly can fly right between the sticky threads of large spider webs. Butterfly wings are covered with up to one-half million scales. They overlap like shingles on a roof. These scales rub off easily. The scales have many interesting jobs. They absorb heat from the sun. They boost the power of the wingbeat. In some butterflies they are shaped like tennis rackets. They give off "perfumes" which the sexes find attractive during courtship.

The butterfly's abdomen is divided into nine segments. A pair of openings on the side of each segment (except the last) lets air enter the body. The air flows through a system of tubes. It contains the oxygen which the butterfly needs in order to live. Inside the abdomen are the digestive organs, and the organs which make the eggs in the female and the sperm in the male.

Migratory Behavior

Like birds, several butterfly species are able to migrate. The most famous butterfly migrant is the *monarch*. Many millions of monarchs fly south from Canada and northern United States in late summer or early fall. Many of these migrants end up in California, Texas and even Mexico! Some individuals make a flight of two thousand miles or more to the same place as past generations of monarchs—even though they had never been there before!

Scientists have studied these migrations for many years. But they still don't know exactly how the monarchs find their way. Most monarchs fly between 10:00 a.m. and 2:00 p.m. on sunny days. Many scientists think that monarchs use the sun to guide them during migration. The monarchs move along the same flight paths year after year. One path is along the eastern shore of Lake Michigan. However, lake storms can be deadly. Hundreds of thousands of dead monarchs have been found washed up on the beach shortly after such a storm. When they reach their winter home, the tired migrants gather in large numbers and roost in pine trees. One favored roost is at Pacific Grove, California. This roost has become a tourist attraction. However, the tourists are fined $500 if they harm a single butterfly. The number of butterflies in a single roost is almost unbelievable. Their bodies are packed so tightly that one cannot see the underlying bark on the trees.

In fact, the combined weight of these butterflies is sometimes so great it causes branches to break.

Scientists were amazed at the size of a monarch roost in Mexico. It was made up of more than 100 million butterflies!

Butterflies, like birds, fly south for the winter. Some fly as far as 2,000 miles.

15

Mating and Egg Laying

Each kind of butterfly has its own kind of courtship and mating. In many the male seeks out a female of his own kind. When a female flies near him, the male can identify her in many ways—by her size, color, shape and the kind of scent she gives off. If she's the right kind of female the male will fly toward the female and rise above her. Then he will start beating his wings very fast. If she doesn't like his courtship, she will fly away. If she likes this attention she will settle down on a nearby leaf. The male will follow her and they will mate.

A short time later the female will look for a place to lay her eggs. It will be a plant which the young caterpillar can use as food. A female monarch butterfly will choose a milkweed plant. Once the right food plant has been found, the female will lay her eggs on the bottom of the leaves.

The female sticks her eggs to the leaves with a juice she makes with a gland in her head. Most eggs are round. However, some are barrel-shaped or pointed. Most eggs are white. But some are orange, red or green. The color and shape depends upon the kind of butterfly which lays them. Most butterfly eggs hatch in just a few days.

Monarch butterfly egg nearing hatching.

Monarch butterfly caterpillar hatching.

Caterpillar climbing out of its egg.

The Caterpillar

The tiny worm-like animal which hatches from the egg is called the caterpillar. They may be smooth and slender and look like tiny snakes, or they may be somewhat flattened. Some are striped or spotted.

Caterpillars protect themselves against spiders, ants, bugs, wasps, lizards, birds, mice and other enemies who would like to eat them. They do this in many ways. Some are colored just like their food plant. This makes it hard for the enemy to see them. Or they may have "false eye" spots or spines that frighten their enemies. Some caterpillars are protected by the bad smells they give off. Some caterpillars are not eaten because they look like little twigs or even like the white droppings of birds!

These two caterpillars have many spots and stripes to frighten their enemies.

The young caterpillar is a real "eating machine." If you ate at the same rate you would put on 20 pounds or more every day!

Caterpillars feed mainly on plants. But they are very fussy about what kind of plants they will eat. Usually it is a plant on which the mother butterfly laid her eggs. A few kinds of caterpillars feed only on insects like ants. The caterpillar crushes its food with a pair of strong jaws found under the head. Other mouth parts are used to taste and smell the food.

Caterpillars have very powerful jaws which they use to crush their food, which is mainly plants.

Six pairs of small eyes are located above the mouth. However, the caterpillar cannot see clearly with them. They can only make out the difference between day and night. A short spinneret sticks out below the mouth. The caterpillar can squeeze a liquid from the spinneret. It hardens at once into "silk."

The part of the body behind the head is divided into 12 parts called segments. The first three form the thorax. Each segment of the thorax bears a pair of short jointed legs. These legs will later be the legs of the adult butterfly. The last nine body segments form the abdomen. It bears five pairs of short false legs. They are lost when the caterpillar changes into an adult. On the sides of the abdomen are small openings. They work very much like similar openings in the adult's body. Oxygen moves through them to the inside of the caterpillar. It is then carried through the body by a system of tubes.

Notice the segments in the body of the caterpillar.

The caterpillar does all the growing for the butterfly. Once the butterfly gets wings, all growth stops. The caterpillar is like a bag filled with fluid. If a hole is made in this bag, the fluid will leak out. This will kill the caterpillar. As the caterpillar feeds, more and more pressure builds up inside the "bag." Finally, the "bag" splits lengthwise. The caterpillar crawls out of the old skin. This may happen four or five times until the caterpillar has stopped growing. Then the caterpillar will spin a little pad of silk on a branch or leaf. It hooks onto the pad with its last pair of false legs. Then it swings out from the leaf with its head pointed down. Now it is ready to change into the next butterfly stage called the pupa.

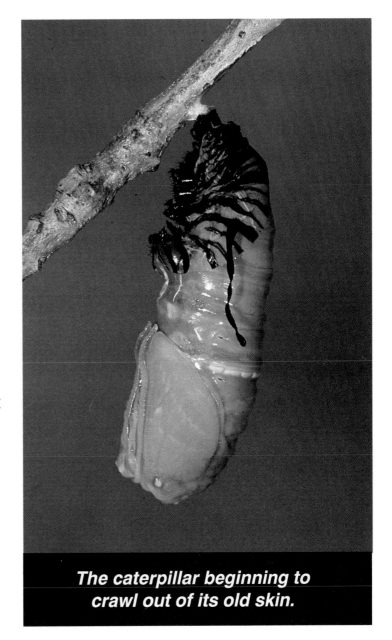

The caterpillar beginning to crawl out of its old skin.

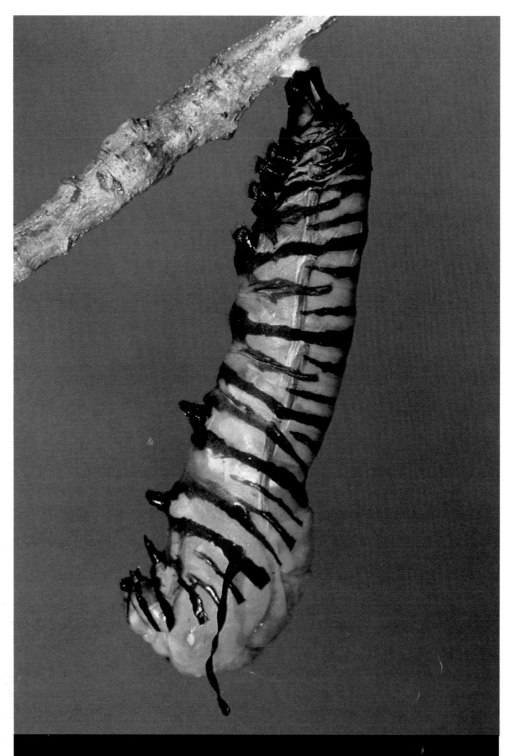

This caterpillar is finally breaking out of its old skin and emerging with a new one.

The Pupa

The body of the caterpillar swells. This causes the old skin to split. The pupa makes wave-like movements and slips out of the skin. Then it hooks into the silk pad with some "claws" at the rear end of its body. It will stay in this position, head down, hanging free, until it turns into an adult.

The pupa stage lasts from ten days to eight months depending on the kind of butterfly. Many pupae may die before they have a chance to turn into adult butterflies. They may be killed by bad weather. Some pupae have false "eye spots" or spines that frighten their enemies away. The pupae of the *mourning cloak* butterfly will thrash back and forth when a hungry enemy gets too close. This may frighten the intruder away. Some pupae look a lot like their background. They have protective shapes or coloration. Some look like dead leaves, twigs or flower petals.

The pupa in its early stage. See how it resembles the leaf it is attached to.

As the pupa matures you can start to see the wings of the butterfly forming inside.

With the warmth of spring, the butterfly breaks out of its pupa prison. This photo shows the butterfly becoming too large for the pupa case.

The pupae of one South American butterfly even looks like the head of a snake, complete with eyes! So instead of gobbling up the pupa, the hungry enemy flies or runs away!

Several kinds of butterfly pupae can make sounds. They do this by rubbing their body segments together. Such rubbing causes clicking, chirping or even humming sounds. These noises may cause pupae-eaters to look elsewhere for their meals.

Because the pupa is almost motionless, some people have called it a "resting stage." Nothing could be further from the truth.

The butterfly finally breaks free and will soon be able to survive on its own.

Feverish chemical activity goes on. Old caterpillar structures like false legs, simple eyes and plant-chewing mouth parts break down. New adult organs like long walking legs, large compound eyes and a nectar-sucking proboscis are built. You could see some of these adult structures under the pupa case.

The increasing warmth of spring is a signal which makes the adult butterfly break out of its pupa prison. The body of the butterfly swells. This causes the pupa case to split. In a short time the adult butterfly crawls out. It's not a very pretty sight. Its wings are crumpled and wet. The body is soft. But soon a dramatic change takes place. The butterfly pumps fluid into its wings. They get larger until they reach normal size. Both wings and body become firm. When the adult is only thirty minutes old, it is ready to take its first flight! Now it can be called "the crown jewel of the insect world." In a short time the butterfly will mate. And this is where our story began. We have followed the life of the butterfly from adult to egg to caterpillar to pupa and back to adult once again. It's an amazing story, don't you think?

The adult butterfly takes flight.

Glossary

Abdomen the rear part of an insect's body which contains the gut and the reproductive organs.

Antennae a pair of long slender structures on the butterfly's head.

Caterpillar the "worm"-like stage of butterfly development.

Compound eye the large insect eye which is made up of thousands of smaller eyes.

Courtship the special kind of butterfly behavior which leads to mating.

Metamorphosis the series of changes in a butterfly's life cycle from egg to adult.

Pupa the stage of the butterfly between the caterpillar and the adult.

Spinneret the silk-spinning organ on the caterpillar's head.

Thorax the middle part of the butterfly's body which bears the wings and the legs.

Bibliography

Douglas, Mathew M. *The Lives of Butterflies.* Ann Arbor: University of Michigan Press, 1986.

Klots, Alexander B. *A Field Guide to Butterflies.* Boston: Houghton Mifflin, 1981.

Sbordoni, Valerio and Severio Forestiero. *Butterflies of the World.* New York Times Books, 1985.

World Book Encyclopedia. Entry on Butterflies. Chicago: Field Enterprises, 1976.

Index

A

abdomen—8, 13, 20
American copper—6
antennae—8, 10

B

birdwing butterfly—4

C

caterpillar—6, 16, 18, 19, 20, 21,
 23, 26
compound eye—8, 26

E

eggs—11, 13, 16, 19

M

metamorphosis—6
microscope—8
migration—5, 14
milkweed butterfly—5
monarch butterfly—5, 13, 14, 15, 16, 17

N

nectar—10, 26
New Guinea—4

P

painted lady—5
pollen—6, 10
proboscis—10, 11, 26
pupa—6, 21, 23, 25, 26
pygmy blue—5

S

scales—13
silk—20, 21, 23
spinneret—20

T

thorax—8, 11, 13, 20, 28
tiger swallowtail—4

W

wing—4, 5, 11, 13, 16, 21, 26

Z

zebra butterfly—11, 13

About the Author

Oliver S. Owen is a Professor Emeritus for the University of Wisconsin at Eau Claire. He is the coauthor of *Natural Resource Conservation: An Ecological Approach* (Macmillan, 1991). Dr. Owen has also authored *Eco-Solutions* and *Intro to Your Environment* (Abdo & Daughters, 1993). Dr. Owen has a Ph.D. in zoology from Cornell University.

To my grandson, Amati,
may you grow up to always
appreciate and love nature.
— Grandpa Ollie